Title
R.L
PTS
TST

D1268415

REAL-LIFE
ZOMBIES

EDGE
BOOKS™

NATURE'S UNDEAD

SNAPPING RATTLESNAKES, FROZEN FROGS, AND OTHER ANIMALS THAT SEEM TO RISE FROM THE GRAVE

BY ALICIA Z. KLEPEIS

CAPSTONE PRESS
a capstone imprint

Edge Books are published by Capstone Press,
1710 Roe Crest Drive, North Mankato, Minnesota 56003
www.mycapstone.com

Cataloging-in-Publication Data
Cataloging-in-Publication Data is on file with the Library of Congress.
ISBN 978-1-5157-2481-0 (library binding)
ISBN 978-1-5157-2508-4 (eBook PDF)

Editorial Credits
Abby Colich, editor; Kyle Grenz, designer; Pam Mitsakos, media researcher;
Laura Manthe, production specialist

Photo Credits
Dreamstime: rahul joseph, cover, Wildphotos, 13; Newscom: Europics, 6, Piotr
Naskrecki/Minden Pictures, 16, Reinhard, H./picture alliance/Arco Images G,
24, Scott Leslie/Minden Pictures, 15; Science Source: Bruce Thomson/ANT Photo
Library, 26, Eye of Science, 18, F. Stuart Westmorland, 14; Shutterstock: Aleksey
Stemmer, 4-5 background, Alon Othnay, 28, Biehler Michael, back cover, Bruce
MacQueen, 29, Cornel Constantin, 10, Cosmin Manci, 22, davemhuntphotography,
8-9 bottom middle, geniuscook_com, 12, Jubal Harshaw, 17, Katarina Christenson,
23, Liew Weng Keong, 11, MarkMirror, 4-5 bottom middle, 21, Matt Jeppson 7,
Matthew R McClure, 27, Michiel de Wit, 20, Photonimo, 1, Sebastian Kaulitzki, 19,
viktori-art, 8

Design elements: Dreamstime

Printed in the United States of America.
009680F16

TABLE OF CONTENTS

THE UNDEAD

It's the dead of winter. On the forest floor, a body lies hidden under leaves and debris. It is mostly frozen.

This strange creature isn't breathing. Its heart isn't beating. One may think this creature is dead. Yet when the weather warms, it comes back to life. Is it a zombie? No, it's a common wood frog, lurking in a North American forest.

Many stories tell of zombies—people who've died and come back to life. In some stories, zombies come back alive by magic or witchcraft. Other stories tell of headless or brainless beings that should be dead, but are alive. Zombies have no control over their own actions. Zombies aren't real. However, many examples of zombielike behavior exist in nature.

Animals such as the wood frog cheat death. They shut down their breathing or other body functions. Other animals lose limbs that keep moving or grow new bodies from *severed* parts. Some zombielike critters move around without brains or heads.

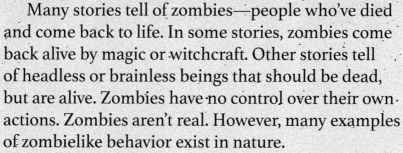

These animals are truly nature's undead.

common wood frog

sever—to cut off

DECAPITATED KILLING SNAKE

Some people find snakes creepy. But a headless snake that still bites? Even creepier! Rattlesnakes, copperheads, and cobras all have this zombielike ability.

In 2014 a chef in China was busy cooking a meal. The dish was to include spitting cobra. A *decapitated* snake lay next to him. For 20 minutes the chef worked. He didn't worry about the dead snake nearby.

decapitate—to cut off the head

Then suddenly, the cobra's unattached head bit the chef.

The chef later died. How did this happen? Once a snake's head is cut off, it's technically dead. Its basic body functions, such as breathing, stop. However, its *reflexes* remain active for up to an hour. The snake has heat *sensors* on either side of its face. The sensors know when another living creature is near. If someone gets too close to the severed head, the snake's reflexes snap into action. The head can still bite and put *venom* into its victim. Sometimes these reptiles even bite their own detached bodies. Why? Biting is the snake's last-ditch effort to survive.

Snakes Playing Dead

Some snakes play dead as a means of defense. The hognose snake flips on its back. It lies still. Its mouth gapes open. Its tongue hangs out. It may vomit or spew blood. If a predator, such as a hawk or a fox, tries to flip the hognose snake over, it flips onto its back again. The snake is trying to ensure its act is believable. It keeps playing dead until it is sure the threat is gone.

reflex—an action that happens without control or effort
sensor—a body part that sends a message to the brain
venom—a liquid poison made by some animals to kill prey

BRAINLESS MOVING FROGS

Ever had someone touch your foot when you weren't expecting it? You probably flinched—fast—without even thinking. Brainless frogs have the same reflex when something touches their feet.

In labs scientists removed the brains of some frogs. The scientists wanted to study how the frogs acted.

Just like brainless zombies, the frogs still moved.

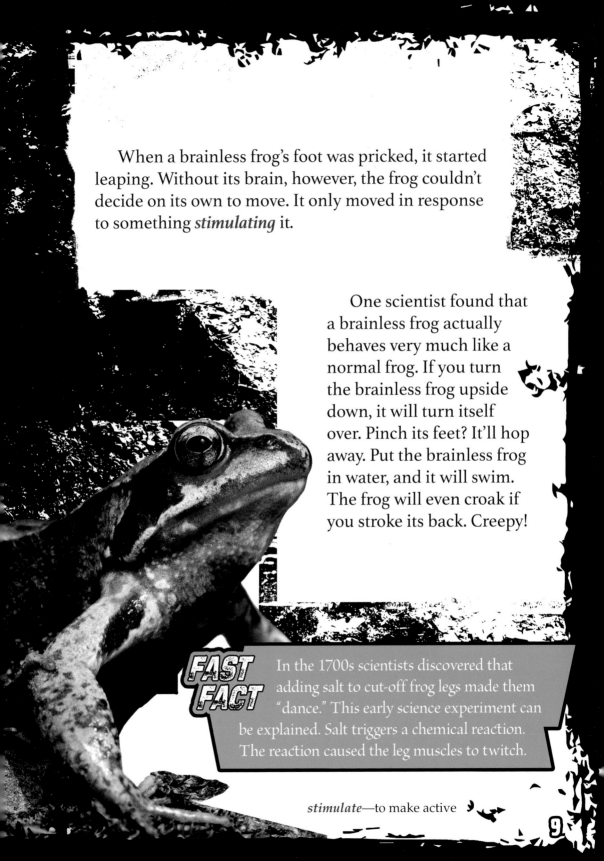

When a brainless frog's foot was pricked, it started leaping. Without its brain, however, the frog couldn't decide on its own to move. It only moved in response to something *stimulating* it.

One scientist found that a brainless frog actually behaves very much like a normal frog. If you turn the brainless frog upside down, it will turn itself over. Pinch its feet? It'll hop away. Put the brainless frog in water, and it will swim. The frog will even croak if you stroke its back. Creepy!

FAST FACT In the 1700s scientists discovered that adding salt to cut-off frog legs made them "dance." This early science experiment can be explained. Salt triggers a chemical reaction. The reaction caused the leg muscles to twitch.

stimulate—to make active

HEADLESS FLIES STILL FLYING

Frogs aren't the only zombielike brainless animals. Inside labs scientists decapitated fruit flies.

The headless flies lived for a day or more.

Seem impossible? These fruit flies have something like a spare brain in their chest. The spare brain manages activities such as breathing, walking, and flying.

Researchers stimulated the fruit flies' *spinal cord* with a laser. This made the brainless flies fly. Brainless flies also responded to light. They moved when lights were flashed on and off. Scientists also say these headless flies learn new things. For example, scientists trained the flies to lift their legs to avoid electric shocks.

Mike the Chicken

In 1945 a Colorado farmer was beheading chickens. The chickens would soon become food for people. Normally, chickens can run around headless for about 15 minutes. Circuits in the spinal cord cause their legs to keep moving. Then they die. But Mike the Chicken (as he became known) lived without a head for 18 months! When decapitating this chicken, the farmer left about 80 percent of Mike's brain behind. This included the parts that control breathing, heart rate, and hunger. Mike the Chicken traveled the country as a zombielike celebrity until he died in 1947.

spinal cord—a thick cord of nerve tissue in the neck and back; the spinal cord links the brain to the body's other nerves

circuit—a path for electricity to flow through

ZOMBIE BODY PARTS

An octopus has lost a fight. It's also lost one of its eight limbs. The cutoff arm still wriggles around. It even senses food nearby. The detached tentacle grabs a fish. Then, like a zombie, it tries to feed its previous owner's mouth. Octopus arms can react for an hour after being cut off. How? Each arm has millions of *neurons*. In other animals, most neurons are in the brain.

But in an octopus, it's as if each arm has a mind of its own.

The octopus won't miss its old limb for long. Soon it will start to *regenerate* its lost arm. An octopus tentacle has *stem cells*. The cells allow new body parts to grow. It takes about 100 days for the new arm to look like the old one.

neuron—a nerve cell that is the basic working unit of the nervous system

regenerate—to make new

stem cell—a cell from which other types of cells can develop

Octopuses aren't the only creatures that can regrow body parts. Salamanders and some lizards detach their tails when threatened. Dropped tails flip, lunge, and jump, confusing the predator. Meanwhile, the animal makes a getaway. With the help of stem cells, the salamanders and lizards grow back their lost tails. In addition to tails, newts and salamanders can regrow lost limbs.

The area where the limb was lost closes. New bones, nerves, muscles, and skin grow.

FAST FACT Once its predator is gone, a lizard often comes back and eats its shed tail. It gets energy from the fat inside.

ONE BODY PART,
ONE NEW BODY

While some animals are regrowing a lost limb, others are growing a whole new body!

A few animals can grow a new body from just a piece of its former self. If a sea star's limb gets torn off, a new arm grows in its place. However, a few species of sea stars can build a brand new body. All a sea star needs is a severed limb with a bit of the central disc—the animal's brainlike center. Stem cells in the central disc help the new body grow. Other creatures also have this death-defying ability. If a piece of a sea sponge gets ripped or broken off, the piece may grow into a totally new sponge.

A New Head for Snail Fur

When tiny snail fur lose their heads, they don't die. These sea creatures grow brand new ones! Snail fur live on the backs of hermit crabs along the coasts of Ireland and Britain. Fish swim by and chomp off snail fur heads as an on-the-go snack. But the snail fur doesn't die. A few days later, they grow brand new noggins. Just like octopuses and sea stars, snail fur have stem cells. The stem cells allow new heads to form.

snail fur on the shell of a hermit crab

THE INCREDIBLE PLANARIAN

The planarian is a type of freshwater worm. It's sometimes called a flatworm. Its regeneration abilities are almost magical. A planarian stays alive even if it is sliced apart.

planarian

It can form a whole new body from just a sliver of its original self!

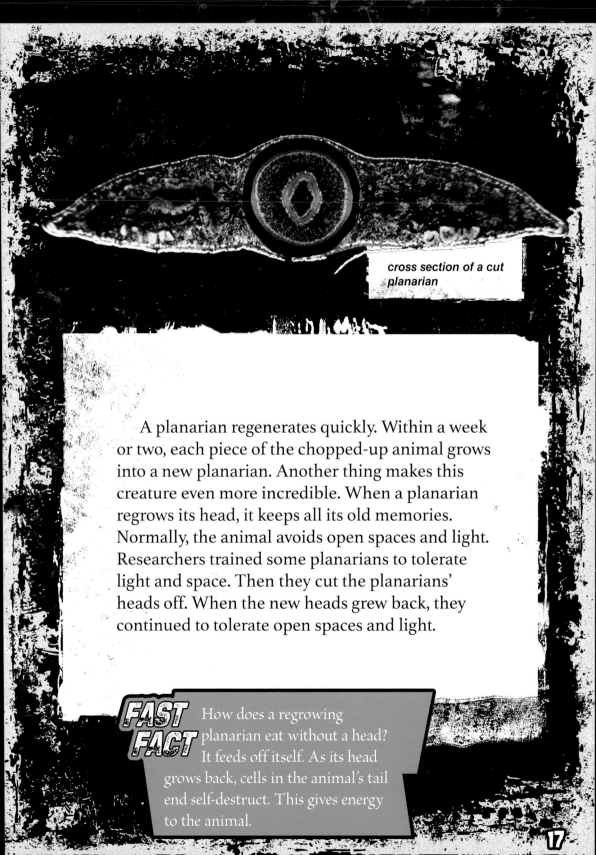

cross section of a cut planarian

A planarian regenerates quickly. Within a week or two, each piece of the chopped-up animal grows into a new planarian. Another thing makes this creature even more incredible. When a planarian regrows its head, it keeps all its old memories. Normally, the animal avoids open spaces and light. Researchers trained some planarians to tolerate light and space. Then they cut the planarians' heads off. When the new heads grew back, they continued to tolerate open spaces and light.

FAST FACT How does a regrowing planarian eat without a head? It feeds off itself. As its head grows back, cells in the animal's tail end self-destruct. This gives energy to the animal.

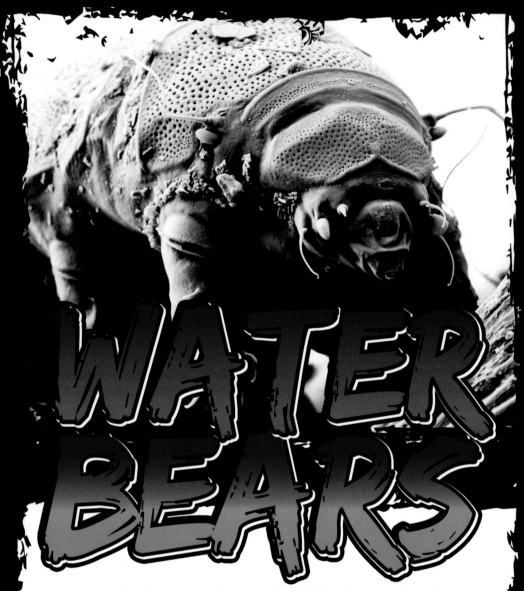

WATER BEARS

One animal can survive in a bubbling hot spring. It can live on a cold mountaintop. It also survives rapid temperature changes. It lives through the drying of its habitat. And it can come back to life after years of *dehydration*. This zombielike creature is the water bear. The tiny water bear is only 0.06 inch (1.5 millimeters) long. It has a large snout and tiny legs with claws.

dehydration—the condition of not having enough water

Biologists call water bears the "hardiest animals on Earth."

When conditions are harsh, a water bear slows down its *metabolism*. It shuts down all of its body functions. Scientists often cannot measure any activity. The creature seems to be dead.

During this state, a water bear loses almost all of its body water. It curls up into a tiny lump. Without water, freezing can't damage the body. A water bear can stay in this state for decades. When it comes back into contact with water, it is completely lifelike once again.

 FAST FACT In 2007 water bears became the first animal to survive a trip to space. They endured subzero temperatures, solar winds, and a space vacuum with no oxygen.

metabolism—the process of changing food into energy

POPSICLE FROGS

In the dead of winter, temperatures plummet. A frog is frozen solid. Later it will bounce back from a near-death state, just like a zombie rising from the dead.

Wood frogs are the only frogs to live as far north as the Arctic Circle. They have a rare trait that allows them to survive being frozen. As the weather becomes cold, a wood frog holes up in the ground. About two-thirds of the water in its body freezes. The rest of the water inside the frog stays liquid. The frog's liver produces a substance that works like the *antifreeze* in a car. This substance limits how much ice can form in the frog's body. It stops the frog from completely freezing to death.

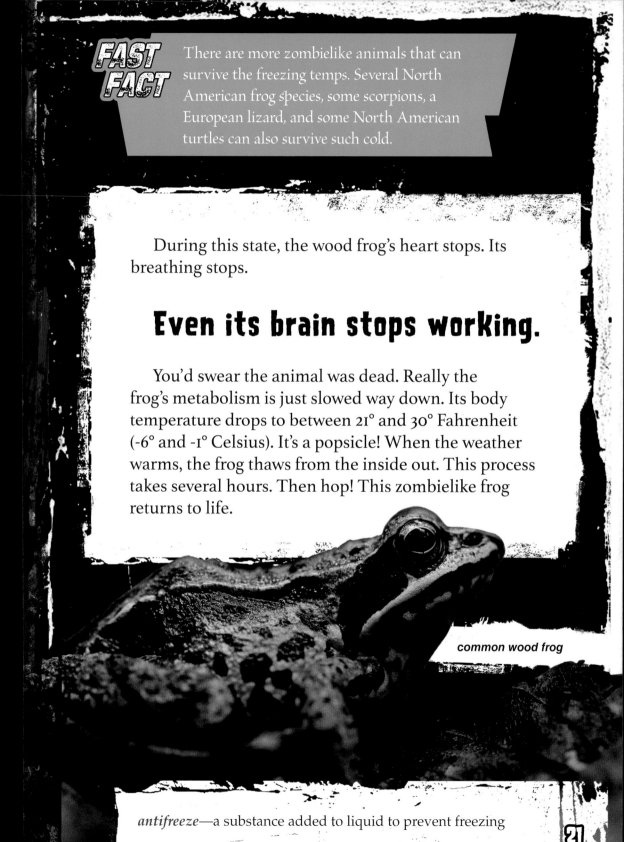

There are more zombielike animals that can survive the freezing temps. Several North American frog species, some scorpions, a European lizard, and some North American turtles can also survive such cold.

During this state, the wood frog's heart stops. Its breathing stops.

Even its brain stops working.

You'd swear the animal was dead. Really the frog's metabolism is just slowed way down. Its body temperature drops to between 21° and 30° Fahrenheit (-6° and -1° Celsius). It's a popsicle! When the weather warms, the frog thaws from the inside out. This process takes several hours. Then hop! This zombielike frog returns to life.

common wood frog

antifreeze—a substance added to liquid to prevent freezing

FROZEN INSECT ZOMBIES

Two insects can survive some of the coldest temperatures on Earth. One is the fungus gnat. This insect gets through the frigid Alaska winter in a bizarre way. Half of the gnat's body freezes. The other half, including its head, remains thawed. How is this possible? This insect floods its body with its own antifreeze. The abdomen of this gnat freezes at -26°F (-32°C). Meanwhile, its head resists freezing temperatures down to -60°F (-51°C).

The *larvae* of Alaska's red flat bark beetle are also extreme survivors. These grubs can withstand temperatures of -238°F (-150°C). The fluids inside these larvae don't freeze. Instead they turn into a glasslike substance. This protects the larvae from any damage. When the temperatures warm up, their bodily fluids return to normal.

The Smallest Zombies

The fungus gnat and the red flat bark beetle aren't the only tiny life forms that can survive freezing. Scientists have brought bacteria back to life. The bacteria came from the bottom of the Guliya ice cap in western China. They are estimated to be about 750,000 years old. In 2009 scientists in Canada brought 400-year-old moss back to life. The moss had been trapped beneath thousands of tons of Teardrop Glacier's ice.

larva—a stage of an insect's life between egg and adult

MUD AND MUCUS ZOMBIES

While some of nature's zombies rise from the frozen ground, others emerge from dry conditions.

lungfish

The African chironomid is one dry survivor. The larvae of this mosquito-like insect live in small pools of water. If the water dries up, the larvae dry out. When this occurs, the larvae mix their *saliva* with soil. They use the mud to build a nest. The nest protects the larvae in this dehydrated state. Then the insects' metabolism stops. They may be mistaken for dead. When rain falls, the zombielike larvae plump back up into their original state.

In western and southern Africa's swamps and backwaters, the zombielike lungfish rises from deadly drought. During the hot, dry summer, the lungfish wiggles into the mud. Then it makes a thin layer of *mucus* around itself. The mucus dries. It leaves a cocoon around the lungfish. The cocoon encases all but the animal's mouth. A little passage for breathing air opens to the surface. The lungfish stays here until water returns. While underground, its metabolism drops. The fish can live in its cocoon for up to a year. When water returns, the lungfish rises to the surface. It gulps up air. The lungfish moves sluggishly at first. Soon it's back to swimming in the water.

va—the clear fluid in the mouth

cus—the slimy, thick fluid that coats the inside of breathing passages

SPENCER'S BURROWING FROG

In Australia's Red Center, daytime temperatures can reach 113°F (45°C). Spencer's burrowing frog can survive in this harsh environment. How?

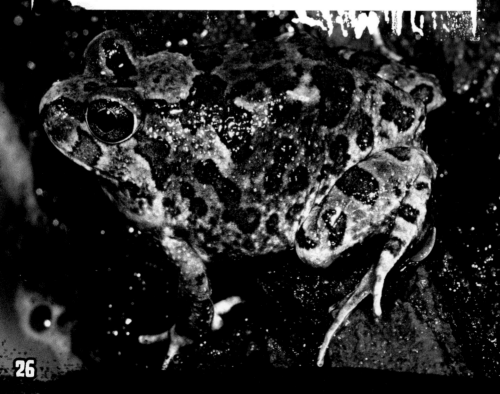

It "zombifies" itself.

When it's dry outside, the frog uses its back feet to dig into the sand. Since moisture is tough to find, this clever critter travels deep down until it finds wet soil. The frog survives by entering *torpor*. It slows its heart rate and breathing way down. It can remain in this zombielike state for years. When rain returns, this frog pops out from its underground hiding spot. It quickly hops away to find food.

The Zombie Plan

The resurrection fern lives throughout the southeastern United States. During a dry period, this pl loses around 75 percent of its wat It shrivels into a gray-brown, dead-looking clump of leaves. Whe rains, this plant springs back to li It looks healthy and green once ag In 1997 the resurrection fern trave into space on the shuttle *Discover* Scientists watched its "resurrecti in zero gravity conditions.

resurrection fern

torpor—a state of lowered body functions
due to poor environmental conditions

DROWN-DEFYING SPIDER

In a lab a wolf spider is trapped. It's in a container filled with salt water. It tries to escape, but can't. The container is covered with wire mesh. Eventually, the spider goes limp. It looks dead. More than a day and a half later, scientists release the spider. At first the spider doesn't move.

Then, like a zombie rising from the dead, the creature starts to twitch.

How did the spider survive underwater for so long? The marsh-dwelling wolf spider goes into a state like a *coma*. In this state the spider switches from using oxygen to not using oxygen. This saves energy for its body's vital functions. Just hours after "drowning," a wolf spider is back on its eight legs.

If you see a spider or snake or frog that you think is dead, don't be so sure. A bodiless limb that's still moving? You know how that happened!

In nature zombielike creatures really do exist!

opossum playing dead

Opossum Coma

Many animals play dead when trying to escape a predator. When threatened, the opossum's performance just might be Oscar-worthy. But biologists think that this may not be a total act. The animal may actually pass out from the stress of an approaching predator. When this happens, its lips draw back. Foam forms around its mouth. It also releases a foul smell. The smell helps the predator think that the opossum is dead. It can take the opossum up to 4 hours to recover from this state.

coma—a state of deep unconsciousness from which it is very difficult to wake up

GLOSSARY

antifreeze (ANT-uh-FREEZ)—a substance added to liquid to prevent freezing

circuit (SUHR-kuht)—a path for electricity to flow through

coma (KOH-muh)—a state of deep unconsciousness from which it is very difficult to wake up

decapitate (di-KAP-uh-tate)—to cut off the head

dehydration (dee-hy-DRAY-shuhn)—the condition of not having enough water

larva (LAR-vuh)—a stage of an insect's life between egg and adult

metabolism (muh-TAB-uh-liz-uhm)—the process of changing food into energy

mucus (MYOO-kuhss)—the slimy, thick fluid that coats the inside of breathing passages

neuron (NOO-rahn)—a nerve cell that is the basic working unit of the nervous system

reflex (REE-fleks)—an action that happens without control or effort

regenerate (re-JEN-uh-rayt)—to make new

saliva (suh-LYE-vuh)—the clear fluid in the mouth

sensor (SEN-sur)—a body part that sends a message to the brain

sever (SEH-vuhr)—to cut off

spinal cord (SPY-nuhl KORD)—a thick cord of nerve tissue in the neck and back; the spinal cord links the brain to the body's other nerves

stem cell (STEM SELL)—a cell from which other types of cells can develop

stimulate (STIM-yew-late)—to make active

torpor (TORE-puhr)—a state of lowered body functions due to poor environmental conditions

venom (VEN-uhm)—a liquid poison made by some animals to kill prey

READ MORE

Goldsworthy, Steve. *Zombies: The Truth Behind History's Terrifying Flesh-Eaters.* Monster Handbooks. North Mankato, Minn.: Capstone Press, 2016.

Hirschmann, Kris. *Real Life Zombies.* New York: Scholastic, 2013.

Larson, Kirsten W. *Zombies in Nature.* Mankato, Minn.: Amicus Ink, 2016.

INTERNET SITES

FactHound offers a safe, fun way to find Internet sites related to this book. All of the sites on FactHound have been researched by our staff.

Here's all you do:

Visit *www.facthound.com*

Type in this code: 9781515724810

 Check out projects, games and lots more at
www.capstonekids.com

INDEX